CHOSEN

Antonette and Christopher

The Beginning……September 2004

Antonette sat on her knees next to her bed, the sunlight barely shining through her burgundy curtains. Antonette's hands cupped to her forehead as she murmured her prayers of protection for her family. Antonette was a 22-year-old African American woman. She was pecan brown, five feet two, and one hundred and twenty pounds. She had shoulder length jet black hair that she took very good care of with her bi-weekly salon visits. Antonette was a small build woman, but curvy since she had two kids and was married by the age of twenty-one years old. She was super responsible, resourceful, and self-assured. Antonette was no non-sense, practical, focused, and ambitious. She attended the local university pursuing her bachelor's degree in business management. She also attended church on a regular basis. Antonette was a strong praying young woman and the foundation of her small family.

Antonette popped up from her knees and walked quickly into her children's room to wake her son up for school. She sat at the foot of her son's bed and stroked his hair, "CJ," Antonette whispered, "It's time to wake up." CJ was their five-year-old son. He was the color of honey with eyes as wide as walnuts. CJ sat up in his bed wearing spider-man pajamas. He walked behind his mom towards the bathroom to brush his teeth. Antonette quickly glanced over in her daughter's crib to make sure she was still asleep before guiding CJ to the bathroom. CJ grabbed his toothbrush and his mother applied the toothpaste for him.

Antonette hurried back to her bedroom so she could wake her husband up for work. She pounced on the bed beside him, her husband turned over groaning loudly. She kissed him on the lips and mumbled jokingly, "Maybe you should join your son in the bathroom for some morning oral hygiene." "Oh really?" Christopher murmured back, "I think that's just the smell of your horrible dinner still on my breath from last night," as he squeezed her supple bottom. The two giggled softly and kissed again as Christopher rolled on top of Antonette in a short-lived make-out session, just as CJ entered the room. "Eeeeeeeeew!" CJ exclaimed. "Alright, alright, alright," said Antonette as she climbed out of bed and hurried towards CJ. "Let's get you dressed!" She looked back over her shoulder flirtingly at her husband and said, "You too sir, get up!"

Christopher groaned and laid on his face for a few minutes before finally sitting on the side of the bed. Christopher grabbed his cigarettes, stood up, and stretched. He walked through his dimly lit house with the cigarette dangling from his mouth. He peaked his head in his son's room to greet him. "Good morning Bighead," Christopher muttered. "Good morning Bighead!" CJ called back to him with a big grin on his face. Christopher strolled into the kitchen wearing nothing but his boxers. He stood in front of the fridge briefly staring at all the upcoming bills Antonette had posted to the fridge to keep the family finances organized and paid on time.

Christopher was blue collared, but a dreamer nonetheless. He was a smooth talker who could get any job he set his mind to. His sisters playfully called him "MacGyver" because he was a "Jack of all trades," and could fix anything. Antonette fell in love with his edginess, confidence, and his ability to woo her at any given moment. Christopher worked as a car salesman. He was an alpha-male with a heart of gold. He was extremely generous and would give the shirt off his back to a stranger. Christopher developed a soft spot for Antonette very shortly after they met. She was the type of woman he felt fit the picture-perfect image he had for his future. Antonette was smart, sexy, spiritual, driven, and in Christopher's mind, the completion of his dreams.

Christopher stood on the front porch of his home, smoking a cigarette and admiring their new neighborhood. The neighborhood was quiet and family oriented. He and Antonette had recently moved into a cute small two-bedroom home. It was canary yellow with white shutters on the outside. The house had a paved driveway, front and back yards for their children to play in. It had been newly remodeled with fresh paint, hardwood floors, new carpet, cabinets, and countertops. In the past, the couple struggled to find a house that they both loved. They needed an affordable price, and a house nice enough to raise two small children. Several months earlier, the couple stumbled upon this small jewel in the middle of the city, being rented out by a woman who gave them a great price. Christopher and Antonette were finally comfortable.

Christopher watched as the kids gathered at the bus-stop while he smoked his morning cigarette. He was

African American, five feet nine with a slim muscular build. Christopher's skin tone was a shade lighter than Antonette. He was rugged, but handsome. Growing up Christopher had a much lighter skin complexion, however, due to spending many years living on the streets as a teen in Miami and working outside as a car salesman, Christopher became much darker over the years.

Christopher was carefree and lived life on the edge. He craved excitement and took risks. That was the ice cold polar opposite of Antonette. She craved stability, security, and structure.

Christopher and Antonette had very different backgrounds growing up. However, they both suffered emotional trauma during their childhoods, which is why they connected on a deep emotional and spiritual level. Antonette's parents were divorced by the time she was six. Her mother was an extremely religious woman who believed deeply in the constitution of marriage. However, she did not have the best choice in husbands. Antonette's first stepdad physically abused her and her younger sister repeatedly.

Christopher's childhood was plagued with heartache because he was born to a teenage mother. Christopher's father was a drug addict and committed suicide when Christopher was only two years old. Christopher was raised by his grandmother since the age of ten. His mother suffered from schizophrenia, she disappeared, and left him and his three younger sisters behind. Christopher ran away from home at sixteen. He and his grandmother clashed regularly. Christopher did not feel loved by her. She was overwhelmed due to the burden associated with the task of caring for seven children at once; three of her own and four grandchildren.

The dysfunction both Christopher and Antonette experienced as youths, gave them both reason to be equally committed to their goal of attaining the "American Dream" for themselves and their two young children; (Cadence) one years old, and (Christopher Junior) five years old.

Antonette and CJ exited the house hurrying past Christopher towards the bus-stop. "Really Christopher?" She asked while not missing a step. "What?" Asked Christopher puzzlingly. "Put some clothes on!" Antonette whispered with a grin. "And deprive the world of my sexiness?" Christopher joked back with a sly grin on his face. Antonette continued walking CJ to the bus stop shaking her head at her husband's over-inflated ego. "Have a good day son, love you!" Christopher shouted, as he threw his cigarette over the porch and headed back inside to get dressed for work. Christopher stood in the doorway of his closet looking around clueless of what to wear. Antonette re-entered the house and bedroom a few moments later. "Your clothes are on the ironing board," she called out to Christopher from the bedroom doorway as she walked out of the room to start breakfast. Christopher made an "about face" military style motion with his feet as he grabbed his clothes from the ironing board and began dressing for work.

Antonette placed her husband's breakfast on the table as she smiled to herself, "Life is good," she thought. "Thank-you Jesus," Antonette mumbled. She felt that her family had a bright future, but for now she was enjoying the space they were in.

Megan, Blake, and Carlos

Megan drives home in her car rapping along to a "Lil Wayne" song. She worked nights as a registered nurse and was headed to her mother's house to get her son ready for school. Dressed in baby blue nursing scrubs, she rapped loudly along with the car radio as she sat in traffic. Being a nurse was sometimes stressful for her, so Megan would use the drive home to try and de-stress before she picked up her son in the mornings.

Megan was a 29 year old Caucasian woman with long wavy blonde hair, slightly chubby but in the right places. She was five feet nine and one hundred and seventy-five pounds. Megan was pretty and a hard worker. She graduated at the top of her nursing class.

She had brains and beauty, however, her taste in men was not very impeccable. Megan's mother, Diane, said she would stop keeping Megan's son if she continued to stay in her last abusive relationship. They had only broken up a month ago and he was still contacting her against her wishes. Megan moved out of the apartment they shared together. She had also changed her phone number, but he still managed to find ways to contact her. The couple dated for six years and also had a son, (Blake) who was five.

Megan pulled up to her mother's home and used her key to get inside. Blake met her at the door with a huge hug. "Hey, you're up early!" Megan said to Blake. "I was waiting for you mommy!" Blake exclaimed. Blake had dark brown curly hair and long curved eyelashes. He had tanned skin, and his curly brown hair was always wild and in his face. His eyes were permanently bright with excitement despite all he and his mother had been through. Megan found herself consistently in awe of Blake's resiliency.

Megan got Blake dressed for school and then went into her mother's bedroom to speak to her before leaving. Megan's mom was sitting on her bed reading her bible with her feet crossed. Megan peeped her head in the door, "Hey mom," said Megan. "How was your night?" Megan's mom Diane answered her dryly in one-word answers without looking up from her reading. She responded "Hey" and "Good" to Megan's greeting and question. Diane was not happy that Megan was a single mother. She felt that Megan was consistently making bad decisions when it came to her choice in men and friends. Diane had issues with letting go and allowing Megan to be an adult. Diane was also a single mom while raising Megan.

She held onto a lot of guilt because she worried about providing a stable life for Megan. Megan was an only child and had to outgrow being spoiled when she became a mother herself.

Megan was aware of her mother's displeasure about her life choices. She never stuck around long when she came to pick up Blake from her mother's house because Diane would often lecture her about the past. Megan thought that her mother was irrational as she could not change the past. "Thanks ma! I'll lock up," Megan called out as she left to take Blake to school.

As Megan arrived at the elementary school she immediately noticed a dark colored car with very dark tint in the parking lot. The car had a government issued tag on it. Megan only noticed the car because the tag was like the tag her ex-boyfriend Carlos had on his car while they were dating. Megan dismissed it and walked her son to the school entrance. As she did, she thought to herself that Carlos could not be so stupid as to violate the restraining order, but then again, he was very cocky because he knew he had friends at the police station and courthouse. Megan had gotten a restraining order against her ex because he had threatened her after she broke up with him. Megan had been receiving ongoing text messages and calls repeatedly until she changed her number a few weeks ago. She was relieved that he could not call anymore, however she felt uneasy not being able to monitor his mental stability on a daily or weekly basis.

Megan exited the school after walking her son to class. Just before she unlocked her car door to get inside she heard a familiar voice call her name.

Megan turned around only to see her ex Carlos standing ten feet away. "What are you doing here?" Megan replied firmly. "I was dropping off my friend's kid," said Carlos. "Can I just talk to you for five minutes please?" Carlos pleaded. "Hell no!" Megan shouted. "I have said all I want to say to you and if you come any closer I will scream!" Megan replied with her voice getting increasingly louder and more hostile. She thought to herself maybe if she sounded tough it would make him feel as though he should fear what she was capable of. "I miss you," said Carlos. "If I see you again Carlos, I'm calling the police and you will be in violation," Megan warned. "How is Blake?" "Does he miss me?" asked Carlos disregarding Megan's threats. Megan became more agitated and her voice level increased as she yelled. "You don't care about Blake!" "Don't even say his name!" Megan remembered how Carlos never spent any time with Blake, and how he would verbally and physically abuse them both. Blake was afraid of his father and Megan was not going to force him to have a relationship with him.

Megan was extremely emotional as she got in her car and sped away as fast as she could. She could not believe that Carlos showed up at the school. She contemplated calling the police, but she knew that Carlos would find a way around being arrested since he knew most of the police department due to him being a detective. Megan was emotional as she drove home. She was planning a move to a new city but was waiting for her nursing contract to be up at the hospital where she worked, then she would move at the end of the month. She contemplated getting a gun. Megan wore mace around her wrist everywhere she went. Her town was small, and she did not feel safe no matter what measures she took.

Carlos stood in the parking lot watching as Megan drove away. He thought he could feel his heart breaking in his chest every time she rejected him. He had been attending anger management classes and doing everything she asked him to do. He knew he had been illogical, mean spirited, and took their family for granted when they were together. However, Carlos knew how much he loved his family and wanted them back together. He had no plans of giving up on them.

Carlos was a gorgeously statuesque man. He was six foot-three and two hundred and twenty pounds of pure muscle. He was ripped with broad shoulders, dark curly hair with deep brown eyes. To top it off, he had dimples in each of his cheeks and big bright pearly white teeth. Whenever he smiled, which was not often, he would stop traffic with the ladies. Even though women would throw themselves at Carlos, he was always a one-woman man. Carlos was an even cuter kid that got everything he wanted. He was from a two-parent home. His parents were immigrants from Puerto Rico, but they worked harder than most to make sure he and his younger brother had everything they needed. Carlos longed for the type of love he witnessed between his parents. When his parents were not at work, they were inseparable.

In high school, Carlos was the captain of the football team. After high school, he played one year in the NFL before he hurt his knee. He was the quarter back of his team. During practice one day he tore a ligament and was told he would need many surgeries just to be able to walk properly. He became depressed for years before he met Megan. Carlos felt that the day he met Megan everything in his life turned around for the better. She encouraged him to get his life back on track. Carlos then pursued his second dream of working in law enforcement. He had only made detective a year ago and that is when their relationship took a turn for the worse. Carlos began working around the clock and came home more stressed out than before. Pressures to be a great detective made him very anxious. He never wanted to fail at anything ever again.

Carlos walked to his car, sat inside and sobbed with his head on the steering wheel. He said a prayer out loud, "God, how can I get her back?" "Please help me get her back!" Carlos pleaded. After a few minutes, Carlos gathered himself as he remembered he needed to be at work shortly. On his drive to work, Carlos saw a billboard ad with a giant diamond engagement ring. The writing on the billboard read, "Propose to Her." Carlos took that as his sign from God. He made a mental note, that day after work he would go ring shopping. Carlos thought to himself, Megan would see that he is serious about making changes and giving her the life, she deserved.

Antonette and Christopher

Christopher sat at his desk at the car dealership. The young couple sitting across from him appeared nervous as they continuously looked at each other every time Christopher would ask them a question about their finances. Christopher had struggled financially in his own young marriage, so he had an especially soft spot for young couples. He would often go above and beyond to help people with their loan applications, so they could get what they wanted and needed. Christopher had even put himself down as a reference a few times. Christopher wanted to help as many people as he could to have the life they dreamed of. He felt the more he helped others then life would somehow work out for him and his family.

"It will take twenty-four hours to get an approval on your application," Christopher stated to the young couple. "Since it's so late in the day just give me a call tomorrow afternoon and I should have some great news for you." The young couple appeared excited as they shook Christopher's hand and walked towards the door to leave. Christopher loved what he did. He saw every couple that came in like he saw him and his own wife.

Christopher began closing the dealership. It was common for him to leave last every day because he was the manager at only twenty-five years old. As one of Christopher's coworkers headed for the door he called back to Christopher, "Hey we're hanging out tonight, you should come this time," said the coworker. "You know the wife ain't having that." Christopher responded with a chuckle. "Well if you change your mind, you know where we'll be." Christopher's coworker replied before exiting the building. Christopher locked up the office and headed home to see his family. He was always happy to go home at the end of each day and report how many cars he sold.

Antonette picked up the two children from the babysitter's house and rushed home to make dinner. She held the phone on her shoulder chatting with her sister as she did daily. She and her sister were very close. What they went through as children made them cling to each other more. The two kept up with each other's lives and confided in one another when they needed someone to lean on. Antonette brought the kids inside holding her one-year old daughter (Cadence) on her hip, while CJ trailed two feet behind her. She put the two children in the living room, in front of the television, with a bowl of popcorn while she started dinner, all the while still chatting and laughing with her sister. They were both married and enjoyed gossiping and talking about the everyday struggles and triumphs of married life.

Although Antonette was happily married, she and Christopher still had their struggles. Christopher struggled with substance abuse and impulse control. He would often make big purchases without consulting Antonette or he would drink alcohol too heavily and have to catch a cab home. Antonette did not like the drinking or the smoking because she was a Christian woman. However, she loved Christopher, so she was willing to take life as it came to make her marriage work.

Antonette was finishing up dinner when she heard the front door open and the children begin to shout. She thought to herself, "That must be Christopher". The children were always excited when their father came home. Antonette stood in the kitchen doorway watching as her two children jumped all over their father. Christopher fell to the floor relishing in the attention and love he got when he came home from work. His five-year old son trying to wrestle him and his one-year old daughter trying to get in on the action by putting Christopher's head in a bear hug and squeezing with all her might. Christopher laughed hysterically at the sight of his children trying to man handle him with such determination. He eventually rose from the floor and carrying both children at the same time throwing them on the sofa. The children screamed out in excitement. Antonette laughed and shook her head in disbelief of the rapport he had built with the children. Their relationship was all their own. In that moment, Christopher locked eyes with Antonette, he walked over to her and they engaged in a long passionate kiss and embrace. The kids shouted in disgust and ran out of the room. "I got three and a possible sale today babe," Christopher whispered in Antonette's ear. Talking about his success was a form of "four-play" for the couple. He knew that every victory at work brought them one step closer to becoming home owners and living the life they dreamed about. They both wanted a better neighborhood and better schools for the children. Although they were grateful, they never stopped believing they could have better in this life. Antonette sat the kids at the table and offered Christopher a plate. Christopher declined stating that he was going to shower first. With a devilish grin he said he would like his dinner in the shower. Antonette knew what that meant. While the kids ate dinner, Christopher and Antonette, snuck off to the shower for a quick love making session.

After dinner Antonette put the kids to bed. It was only eight o'clock so she and Christopher sat in bed talking. Christopher mentioned that he had been invited out for drinks by his co-workers. Antonette stared him in the eyes as she responded, "And?" "And I kinda wanna go," Christopher replied nervously. "Christopher," said Antonette. "Last time you got too drunk and couldn't drive home." "I don't want that to happen again," Antonette said in a warning voice. "I won't this time babe, I promise." Christopher pleaded. "I just want to be respected at work." "They think I'm a goody goody." "I just want to build a little team spirit." "Besides, it's good for business when we all get along, you know, good energy!" Christopher added. Antonette reluctantly agreed. She wanted her husband to be happy regardless of how she felt about his going out. I won't be gone long babe," Christopher kissed Antonette on the cheek as he rushed out the door. "Love you!" Shouted Christopher. "Love you too," Antonette mumbled as she heard the door shut while she was speaking. She sighed, said a silent prayer for his safety, and then turned the television on to pass the time.

Christopher arrived at the bar. His coworkers all stood up and cheered. Christopher was immediately filled with excitement at his reception. "Shots on me!" Shouted one of Christopher's coworkers. Everyone cheered and begin throwing back shots. Christopher swallowed his first shot, and then another. Then two more. He thought to himself. I'll just have water and sit for the last hour before going home. "It's just one night." Christopher thought. He knew he had no plans of making a habit of hanging at bars with his coworkers because he and his wife were saving for a house. Christopher was a family man. He often felt out of place when he hung out at bars.

Megan and Blake

Megan and Blake laid in bed as she read him a bedtime story. Megan adored these small moments with Blake. When she and Carlos were together peace wasn't so easy to come by. She overexerted herself emotionally trying to keep Carlos happy. He was moody because he was overworked and tired. He was trying really hard to prove himself at work, so he often came home and took his frustrations out on her and Blake. Megan spent every day since she left Carlos, trying to make up for the damage that she felt Blake suffered emotionally while living in such a volatile environment for so many years.

Megan and Carlos' relationship changed drastically after Blake was born. When the couple first met, Carlos waited on Megan hand and foot. He treated her like a princess. Megan felt worshipped by Carlos. Although he was a bit controlling and did not like any of her friends, Megan was completely taken by how "Dreamy and romantic" Carlos was to her. She quickly fell head over heels in love and spoke to her friends less and less. Whenever she did spend time with her friends it would cause a fight between her and Carlos, so she decided that having a social life outside of him was not worth the trouble. Megan settled into life with Carlos thinking that as long as she did everything right, she could make him happy. Megan began to see how wrong she was when Blake was three years old. Carlos began to get physical with her when he became angry. He would push, slap, and even punch Megan in the face when they got into arguments. The last straw was when Carlos pulled his gun and threatened to shoot her when she said she would leave him. Megan realized then that she could not save Carlos. He had to get help and save himself. Megan cut her losses and was committed to starting over and building a better life for herself and Blake. She had no plans to ever reconcile with Carlos.

Megan finished the bedtime story and kissed Blake on the forehead. "Alright, Goodnight baby," Megan said softly. Blake rolled over and looked at his mom. His eyes were half open. "Mom?" Blake called out, "Night light," Blake added. "I got it," said Megan as she reached into the closet and flipped the light switch up.

Megan sat in her living room looking at apartments on her phone. Planning their future was the only thing that kept her mind from constantly worrying about what Carlos would do next. She feared Carlos, but she didn't think that he was capable of hurting her or Blake. She felt that Carlos wanted to scare her into having things back the way they were. Megan refused to be controlled by him any longer. She and Blake's lives had suffered enough she thought. It was time to be happy again. Megan reactivated all of her social media accounts in order to reconnect with the friends she had cut off over the years. She blocked Carlos on social media, however she was getting requests from strange accounts. Megan knew that Carlos was behind the random requests from strangers. Megan would block the accounts and continue with her planning. Although Megan made many mistakes in the past, she was determined to do better for the sake of her son.

Christopher

Tribulation

Christopher was driving home from the bar. He felt sober as he had stopped drinking two hours before leaving. Christopher hung around drinking water and talking with his coworkers after the gathering was over. They joked around and laughed all night. Christopher had a great time. He could not wait to get home, kiss his kids, and hold Antonette until he fell asleep. He was also very hungry as he didn't eat dinner when he got home from work. His attraction to his young wife made him completely forget about his hunger.

Christopher felt disenchanted at how heavy the rain had gotten. Visibility was not clear, and he could not drive as fast as he wanted to. The whole way home he could hear his wife's voice telling him to be careful. Christopher passed a police car on the road and sat up straighter thinking about how his wife would flip out if he had gotten a DUI. Christopher nervously watched the cop in his rear-view mirror, as he did even when he hadn't been drinking. He knew it did not take much to get pulled over, so he always kept a close eye on passing cops and made sure he was following all traffic laws, at least until they got out of his eyesight.

The police car's red tail lights became smaller and smaller as the car disappeared from Christopher's rearview mirror. Christopher began to relax as he knew he had to take his time getting home. The rain was very heavy and Christopher's windshield wipers were not doing the best job of clearing the rain from the windshield. Christopher made a mental note to buy some new windshield wipers when he got paid again. He relaxed into his seat and reached down to turn up the car radio. The moment Christopher looked up again, a man was stepping off the curb into the path of his car. Christopher pressed his brake all the way to the floor of his car, but the car did not slow in speed. The road was so wet that his car tires did not make a screeching sound that they would normally make when the rubber scrubbed the concrete. The man crashed into the windshield making a large hole, and glass shattered all over the dashboard. The man then rolled off the hood of the car onto the concrete road and the car continued sliding in the heavy rain. Christopher traveled another thirty feet before the car came to a complete stop. He was stunned and in shock. Christopher's breathing was fast and hard as if he was running out of air. He could not believe what just happened. He sat in his car, shouting and banging the steering wheel, "No No No!" Christopher Shouted. "This isn't happening, this IS NOT HAPPENING!" Christopher's voice got increasingly louder as he had begun to panic, feeling fear, and anger. He no longer felt intoxicated, but who would believe him since he had been out drinking. "This was very bad," Christopher thought.

He sat looking in the rearview mirror as all the passing cars around him came to a stop. His thoughts were racing. "What did I do, what did I do?!" Christopher cried out in a voice almost crying while still watching his rearview mirror expecting the police to pull up at any moment. Christopher's eyes welled up with tears as he thought about Antonette. He could feel her disappointment even though she had not been informed of the accident yet. He knew she would be devastated and angry. He thought about how much he would miss his kids when he is locked away for killing someone with his car. Christopher glanced around at the scene. A small crowd was gathering around the man he hit, however his car was far enough away and it was raining hard enough that maybe they could not see his license plate. In that moment, Christopher made the decision to leave. He thought maybe he could still save his own life. He thought to himself that this wasn't even his fault as the man stepped out in front of a moving car. Christopher sped away no longer watching his rearview mirror. He had to get out of sight as quickly as possible. He quickly turned the corner going in a different direction, so he would not give anyone a chance to see his license plate.

Christopher drove along a dark back road brainstorming of what to do. There were very few street lights so he felt he was less likely to be spotted by the cops. There was a very large hole in his wind shield, so he knew that he could not drive very far. He thought to himself, "I will drive the car into the lake, or maybe set it on fire." Christopher drove until he came upon a wooded area. Christopher drove into the trees as far as he could until he thought the car could not be seen from the road. He turned off the car ignition and sat there sobbing. Christopher felt like his life was over and he was going to lose everything; wife, kids, job, and future.

Carlos

Carlos laid in bed scrolling through his old social media pictures as he often did at night when he could not sleep. It was about 11:30 pm on a Tuesday night. Carlos reminisced on how happy his life had been just a brief time ago. He saw how happy he, Megan and Blake looked in the pictures. He reminisced on trips they took and how happy his son Blake was having his parents together. He rolled over and grabbed the ring from his nightstand that he purchased earlier in the evening when he got off work. "I'm going to get you back babe," Carlos murmured. He then turned his attention back to his phone. Carlos went to Megan's social media page. She had blocked him; however, he created a fake page pretending to be someone else and she added him unwittingly. He would monitor her statuses to see how her life was going. He wanted to make sure that she did not move on. He knew that she wouldn't, because they had broken up hundreds of times and always gotten back together. Their relationship was magical, Carlos thought to himself. Just then Carlos's phone rang, and it was his office. He dreaded answering because he knew anytime he got a call this late at night a horrific crime had been committed and he would be up until morning investigating. The best evidence is gathered in the first twenty-four hours while witnesses' memories were fresh. Carlos answered the phone and the dispatcher informed him of a "Hit and run" very close by where Carlos lived. Carlos quickly jumped up, put on his clothes, gun holster, and rushed out of the door.

Carlos pulled up to the address where the "Hit and run" took place. He was greeted by the police on the scene who informed him that a man was just transported to the hospital in critical condition. "It's not looking good," the officer reported. He directed Carlos to a group of witnesses standing next to the road. Carlos walked up to the closest witness who seemed to be the most shaken up. Carlos looked around at the other cars, remembering that the dispatcher said "Hit and run." Carlos then questioned the witness, "Can you describe the car?" "It was red," said the witness. "I can't tell you the model because it happened so fast, it was dark, and it was raining so hard, the car couldn't stop," the witness added. "Then they left?" Carlos asked raising his eyebrows. "Yes, they sat for a minute and then they sped away," answered the witness. "They didn't get out of the car or anything?" Carlos inquired further. "No," the witness answered shortly. "The windshield had a large hole in it," added the witness. "Was the driver male or female?" Carlos asked. "I think it was a man, but I am not sure," the witness replied.

Carlos left the scene and drove around his small town looking for a red car with a broken windshield. He figured whomever the person was, was long gone by now, however, it was protocol. After driving around for an hour Carlos went by the hospital to check on the victim and get information to contact next of kin.

Carlos arrived at the hospital and spoke to the nurse on duty. He was told that the victim was in critical condition, in a coma, and he would be notified once the victim awoke. Carlos inquired whether there was any next of kin listed on his records. The nurse gave

Carlos a few names to call as he left the hospital to search for the red car again before heading home for the night.

Antonette

The Next Morning………..

Antonette tossed and turned in her bed the whole night. Christopher did not come home, and she was extremely worried as this was completely out of character for him. Her mind raced as she played multiple traumatic scenarios that could have possibly happened. She was trying to be strong, but she could feel that something wasn't right. She did not wake her son up for school because she wanted to be prepared for any outcome. Antonette picked up the phone and searched for the number of any of Christopher's coworkers so she could call them and find out where he was. Just as she picked up the phone, it rang. It was Christopher's cell phone number. Antonette answered, feeling slightly angry but relieved that

Christopher was alive. "Antonette," Christopher said with the sound of desperation in his voice. Antonette thought to herself he must be in jail, "But how could he be calling from his cell phone. "Something terrible has happened," continued Christopher. His voice was cracking as if he was going to cry. "What is going on Christopher?" Antonette said with panic creeping up in her voice. "I hit someone babe, I hit them hard." "It's bad, very very bad." "WHAT!" Antonette shouted. "Are you in jail?!" Antonette exclaimed. There was a long pause on the phone. "Christopher!" Antonette continued very loudly forgetting that the kids were sleeping in the next room. "I, I left Antonette, Christopher replied hesitantly. "I was so scared, and I had been drinking, but I wasn't drunk babe I promise you!" "They came literally out of nowhere, so I could not stop." "I tried to stop but the road was wet, and they jumped out in front of my car!" Christopher rambled on frantically. Antonette listened in disbelief at what she was hearing. She repeated what she heard as if she had heard wrong. "So, you're telling me, you hit someone with your car and then left the scene of the accident before the police arrived!?!" "You are not serious right now!" We could lose everything!" Antonette screamed. Antonette dropped to her knees, they both were sobbing at this point. "Did anyone see you?" Antonette stop sobbing long enough to ask. Christopher paused again. "Yes," he answered, "It was so dark, and it was raining, so I don't think anyone could see my car," he continued. "That's beside the point Christopher!" Antonette interjected. "It's not right Christopher!" "It's not right!" Repeated Antonette. "Where is the car?!" "Where are you?!"

Antonette continued. "I hid the car and I called an old friend to come get me," replied Christopher. "I told him I was in trouble." "I didn't tell him what happened." Christopher continued. "What do we do now Christopher?" Antonette asked. "I don't know babe." "I have to figure that out." "I will call you as soon as I figure out what to do," Christopher replied. "When are you coming home?!" exclaimed Antonette. "I don't know babe," Christopher answered. "I don't want to go to prison." Christopher continued still crying on the phone." "I love you Antonette, kiss the kids for me."

Christopher hung up the phone. Antonette fell to her knees sobbing. Her world had instantly flipped upside down. She thought about what could possibly happen next. She was confused, scared, and the saddest she had ever felt in her life. Antonette begin to pray. She prayed for the person Christopher had hit. She prayed for Christopher and for her strength. "It's in your hands God, fix it Jesus!" Antonette cried out. She laid on the floor. Antonette felt as though she could die right there, but she knew she had to be strong for her children. Antonette decided she would not fall to pieces, but she would put on a happy face for the kids. No matter what happened she would shield her children from as much as she could. Antonette continued to lay in the floor praying, awaiting the sound of her kids awakening shortly. She did not want them to see her laying on the floor, yet she did not have the strength to get up.

Carlos and Antonette

Carlos woke up feeling very tired. He had only slept about three hours. He played the details of his new case over and over in his mind as he worked to put the pieces together. He got dressed and headed to his office. He wanted to be in place if any calls came in about the accident. On his way to the office he drove by Megan's mom's house as he usually did. He knew that she would come by there often because her mother kept their son while she worked.

Carlos arrived at the office. He grabbed a cup of coffee as he stood around discussing the details with his fellow detectives. They brainstormed about the type of person that would drive off after hitting someone. They all agreed that the person had to be afraid of going to jail, possibly drunk or high. They even entertained the idea that the person responsible could even be a teenager. At that moment, a woman approached from the news station. She had gotten a tip about the accident and wanted to do a story about the "Hit and run" on the news. Carlos quickly agreed, knowing that getting the public involved could expand his reach, as he wanted to close the case very swiftly. He knew that going on the news would help him to find the damaged car. Carlos stood in front of the reporters and the cameras, as he pleaded with the public for anyone who has seen the damaged car or knew the driver to come forward and do the right thing.

Carlos was sitting at his desk when he received a call from a patrol cop. The cop had found the car in the woods. The cop read the license plate to Carlos before hanging up the phone. Carlos ran the license plate number and the name "Antonette Davis" came up on his computer. He printed out the details and left the office to go and question her about the accident.

Antonette sat in her living room watching television as her two children played nearby on the floor. She was anxious the entire day. She held her phone, waiting to hear from Christopher again but the phone never rang. Just then, there was a knock on the door. Antonette jumped abruptly to her feet and ran to the door hoping it was her husband and he had lost his house keys. She opened the door to see a tall Hispanic man wearing a bullet proof vest and gun on his hip. Antonette was noticeably caught off guard. Their eyes met and they both knew in that moment why he was there. "Can I help you?" Antonette asked through the screen door. "Mrs. Davis?" Carlos began, "Yes," answered Antonette. "Are you Antonette Davis?"

"Yes, I am," Antonette answered again. "I am detective Carlos Gonzales." We found your car this morning and we believe that it is connected to a hit and run that happened last night." "Were you driving that car last night?" "No sir," answered Antonette. "Do you know who was?" the detective questioned. Antonette stared at the detective without answering. The detective continued by stating he knew that she wasn't driving the car and knew it was her husband. He then asked her if her husband was home. Antonette stated that she had not seen Christopher since last night. Carlos asked if she knew where he was. "No," Antonette answered. "Look Mrs. Davis," Carlos replied, "You seem like a good woman." "I am pretty sure your husband did not mean to hit that man, but I need for him to turn himself in." "If you are not careful you could also be arrested for aiding and abetting a criminal," Carlos added. "The victim is in a coma and it doesn't look good." "He might not make it, so right now your husband is looking at a possible vehicular homicide charge," The detective warned. "You weren't in that car, do you want to go down with him?" "Do you want someone else to raise your kids?" threatened the detective trying to scare Antonette into talking. Antonette looked down at the ground as she fought back tears. She knew that not speaking up was wrong, but she also knew that Christopher was a good person and husband, she could not bring herself to speak against him. "He called me okay, but I do not know where he is." Antonette responded feeling relieved that she actually didn't know where Christopher was. She would have no choice but to tell where he was if she knew because she was not willing to allow the children to live without both of their parents.

The detective left his card in the crack of the young couple's door and instructed for her or Christopher to call him when he was ready to turn himself in. The detective then left and arranged for a patrol unit to watch the Davis's home. Since Carlos had confirmed that Christopher was driving the car, he was headed downtown to retrieve an arrest warrant for Christopher's arrest.

Antonette wanted to see Christopher one last time before she would convince him to turn himself in. Antonette was in agony. She no longer recognized her life. She never saw this turn of events coming and was in disbelief of how quickly life had changed. She began praying to God that the man her husband hit did not die. She could not bear the thought of someone dying because of a mistake her husband made. She also could not bear the thought of losing Christopher and becoming a single mother. She felt alone. She did not know who to call or who to talk to. She felt ashamed and she did not want to talk to her family because no one would understand why Christopher did what he did, but Antonette understood. She was just as desperate to hang on to her soulmate and their family as he was to hang onto them. They could not afford a lawyer, and Antonette knew whether the man lived or died, life would never be the same for them again. Antonette hugged her children and held them close. She felt the only thing left in her power to do was love them the best she could, hold on, and pray.

Megan

Megan laid in bed watching her son sleeping next to her. She often got up early, as she never slept well at night anymore. Working nights had ruined her sleep patterns and she also worried a lot about what the future might bring. She worried about Carlos and if he would leave her alone and let her live her life. She knew that he was very much obsessed with her still. She was post-traumatic due to putting up with years of verbal, emotional, and physical abuse. She tried her best not to focus on the past, but it was difficult because she and Carlos still had a visitation hearing coming up in a week and she did not know how she was going to get through it, if she had to see him on a regular basis. She felt in her heart that she was absolutely done with the relationship. She had given him so many chances to go to counseling and get his life together. However, Carlos continued to take her and their son for granted, as if they would always be there by mistreating them both.

Megan woke Blake up for school and got him dressed. She still felt the anxiety from a few days ago when Carlos showed up at their son's school. She was not sure what else she could do other than move out of town. She was going to request permission to move out of state at the visitation hearing. She knew that Carlos would not be happy about it, but it was what she needed.

Megan strapped her mace around her arm and she and Blake headed for the car. She glanced around at the apartment parking lot looking for suspicious cars. She had a feeling that Carlos was always watching her since he would randomly bump into her when she was out and about around town. Megan was as careful as she could be. She felt if she was firm and did not give Carlos any false hope that in the future they could be cordial enough to co-parent if he got counseling for his anger issues.

Megan and Blake headed to his school. She walked him to class and made it back to her car without incident. She was tired of looking over her shoulder and had gotten to the point where nothing was going to stop her from the having the new life she craved so badly. She and Blake were happier than they had ever been, and she was willing to do whatever it took to keep it that way.

Antonette and Christopher

Christopher laid on the sofa at his friend's house. His friend was single, and his apartment smelled of old furniture and cigarette smoke. Christopher's soul ached being away from his family. All he could think about was jail and how much he was going to miss his wife and kids. He was full of regret. He wished he had never gone anywhere the previous night. He just wanted to go back to life before all this happened. He felt like he was in a bad nightmare and he was going to wake up any minute. Christopher laid there trying to figure out what to do next. He thought about running away with his wife and kids to some foreign country. Then he thought about how they barely had enough for plane tickets. When they got to this faraway place, he didn't know how they would eat or find a place to stay. Christopher begin to cry, "Oh God!" Christopher prayed out loud. "I have messed up bad this time God!" "I need you!" "Please help me!" Christopher begged. He dried his tears and then decided he would accept his fate. He would not run. He would not take Antonette and the kids through anything else. He accepted that he was about to spend the next few years of his life in jail, but first he had to see Antonette and his kids one last time.

Christopher waited until it was dark outside before making his journey home. He was nervous and anxious, as he felt the world was looking for him. He had seen the "Hit and run" story on the news and the detective said that they had a lead and did not yet have a suspect in custody. Christopher knew that it wouldn't be long before they were on his trail. He was guilty, and nothing could change that now.

Christopher arrived at his neighborhood and had the driver drop him a block over to be on the safe side. He had been away from Antonette and the kids for twenty-four hours and could no longer stay away from them any longer. He walked through the neighbors' yards and entered his home through the back door that led to the kitchen. His heart was beating out of his chest as he walked through the dark kitchen. He was nervous with anticipation, but terrified of facing his wife after what he had done to their family. Christopher made his way through the barely lit house quietly as he could, knowing his children were already sleeping. He slowly walked to him and Antonette's bedroom door and stood in the doorway. He saw Antonette sitting up in bed watching television. Antonette immediately felt Christopher's presence as she turned to see him standing in the doorway with dread in his eyes. Antonette sprung out of bed and ran to Christopher as fast as humanly possible. She dove into his arms. The couple held each other and wept. They both knew this would be one of the last times they would be able to physically comfort one another. They did not want the moment to end. Antonette wished that she could stop time and live in that moment forever. She knew that morning was coming, and they would have to face the harsh reality of what was going to happen next.

Carlos

Carlos sat in his car at a fast food restaurant parking lot. He had bought dinner but didn't have much of an appetite. He did not like nights because he didn't have much to occupy his mind. Any serious crimes got major attention in that small town and never took long to solve. He often drove around at night looking for Megan. He would drive by her mother's house and by the hospital where she worked. He wasn't going to give up until he could convince her of how much he loved her. He knew he could easily move on and have casual sex with any girl who had been pining after him since high school, but nothing he did took away the heartache he felt deep in his heart. Carlos' emotions would fluctuate from utter sadness to complete anger very quickly when he felt like he wasn't being understood and seen for who he truly was. He tried counseling but did not feel as though it was working. He had missed two weeks in a row and didn't plan to return. He knew that Megan would reconsider their break up once she saw the size of the diamond ring he bought her. He felt this gesture would tell her everything she needed to know about his character and the type of man he was striving to be. Carlos took comfort in plotting his proposal. In his mind, he saw Megan's eyes light up, she would jump into his arms, and he would pick her up and spin her around just like they did in the movies. He smiled to himself as he turned on his car to begin his journey home. Carlos opened the paper bag, took out a hamburger, and began eating. He was feeling like himself again. He knew that he was very close to getting his life back. He could not wait to show

Megan the ring and ask her to be his wife. "I just have to plan it better this time," Carlos said out loud. He had to time the proposal just right so that Megan would see his thoughtfulness and remember the good times and how much they loved one another.

Antonette and Christopher

Antonette woke up the next morning with a bittersweet feeling. More bitter than sweet because Christopher was home in bed with her and the kids, but she knew that at any moment the police could show up and take him away. The couple didn't take one second for granted. They both tried to memorize each moment. Antonette knew at some point they should call the detective, nevertheless, they carried on the day with the children, having breakfast, making love, holding each other, and playing with the kids. Antonette and Christopher were not planning on telling their son where his father was going, however, they wanted to prepare him emotionally for his father's inevitable future absence. Neither of them had a clue of how long that would be. Antonette and

Christopher both agreed that she would not bring CJ to see him in jail or prison. Christopher did not want to be seen powerless to his first and only son.

Christopher told Antonette to find a good man, so she can have support and a good step dad for their kids. Antonette held her head down and wept, knowing that she did not want any other man but him. They had met as teenagers. They weren't serious at first but Antonette became pregnant with their son within six months of dating. They were inseparable from that point on. Christopher vowed that he would always take care of them both no matter what. Antonette fell deeply in love with Christopher. The two married shortly after their son was born. They wanted badly to give him that picture perfect life and childhood neither of them had growing up.

Antonette and Christopher went to bed that night both knowing that tomorrow was the day that they were going to call the detective. It was agony prolonging the call, knowing that the time they had left was quickly passing. They both wanted to get on with it. The couple had watched the news that evening, and the man Christopher hit, who had now been identified as "Henry Taylor," was still in a coma. The two had also learned that the man had to have both legs amputated because they were so severely damaged and could not be saved. This news devastated them both. They were unhappy that Christopher was responsible for hurting someone to that extent. After learning the information, Christopher was ready to face his consequences.

The next morning was very quiet. Christopher sat at the table with his family while they ate but he could not eat. He and Antonette communicated with their eyes. They knew they would call the detective after breakfast. When they were done eating, Antonette took the children to the living room, so Christopher could make the call to the detective. He called detective Gonzalez and told them he was ready to turn himself in. After the call, Christopher joined Antonette in the living room. Christopher and Antonette huddled closely on the sofa bracing for what was coming.

Forty-five minutes later Detective Gonzalez showed up with a small army of at least eight cop cars. Christopher wondered to himself how many cops would have showed up had he not called to turn himself in. Detective Gonzales knocked on the door and Christopher answered. Christopher shook his hand and asked the detective if he could be handcuffed across the street. He did not want to be put in handcuffs in front of his wife and kids. The detective agreed, and he and the other officers waited across the street. Christopher closed the door and hugged his family one last time. He walked out of the door and headed across the street to the awaiting assembly of cops dressed in swat gear. Antonette watched anxiously from the window as if what was about to happen would magically not occur. She watched as they cuffed and put Christopher into the squad car, then drove away.

Antonette went to her bedroom away from the children. She buried her head in her pillow and bawled loudly. She felt as if her heart was being shattered in a million pieces. She cried out, "Why God why!" Why did he not protect them from this? What did she do to deserve this to be happening to her and her children? When she thought of her kids her heart would ache worse. She did not want her children to grow up knowing that their father was in prison for hitting and nearly killing someone with his car.

Antonette had been a faithful woman. She spent most of her young adult life in the church and the God she had become accustomed to, went before her and made every path smooth. Antonette could not make sense of this situation. She sobbed into her pillow until she heard her son's small knock on her bedroom door. She quickly wiped her eyes and gathered herself. In that moment, Antonette remembered God's words. Antonette begin to speak. She said "God, you said that you can do all things, and nothing is too impossible for you." "I need you to come through for us Lord." "Fix this situation." After she finished praying, Antonette got up, and decided it was time to be strong. She knew that she had to put on a poker face for their children.

Megan, Blake, and Carlos

Megan made her way to pick her son up from school as she usually did. She was in good spirits, she was off work that day and had planned to take Blake to the park after school for a picnic. She drove along in her car singing loudly. Megan had not heard from or seen Carlos since last week and finally felt like he was getting the picture. "Finally," Megan thought, "They were going to live in peace." Megan pulled into the school and got her son from class. As they were walking to the car, Megan's heart dropped. Across the parking lot she saw Carlos standing at her car holding balloons and flowers. She and Blake continue to walk to the car slowly. Megan whispered down to Blake to run back into the school if anything went wrong, and they continued to the car, so they could attempt to leave.

Megan arrived at her car, Blake standing at her side holding on to her leg. "What is going on Carlos?" Megan said in a puzzling manner.

"Us," answered Carlos attempting to hand her the flowers and balloons. "I'm ready to be the man you and our son need me to be." "I've changed Megan." "Let me prove it to you!" Carlos said, beginning to sound more desperate by the second. Carlos placed the flowers and balloons on Megan's car, then reached into his pocket, pulled out the engagement ring and got on one knee in front of the frightened pair. "Be my wife!" "Let's be a real family this time." Carlos pleaded. "Are you serious?" Megan asked sounding bewildered. "As a heart attack," answered Carlos. "It's what I want the most in this world," Carlos added. "Oh my God!" Megan said hysterically. "You are crazy!" "You have lost your mind completely if you think I would ever consider marrying you!" "Get in the car Blake!" Megan shouted as she hit the unlock button on her key chain. Just as Blake took a step towards the car, Carlos reached his arm out and blocked the boy's path. "Don't you dare touch him!" Megan shouted with anger in her voice. Blake took a step backwards and again was clinging to his mother's leg. She could feel his grip much tighter now. "Look," Carlos pleaded trying to sound calmer, but his heart was beating out of his chest with the fear that he was still being rejected after all he had done to try and prove his love for her and their son. "Don't do this, let's go have dinner so we can talk about this," Carlos said slowly getting to his feet. He put the ring back in his pocket hoping that his new slower approach was working. "Get out of our way Carlos!" Megan said in a threatening tone of voice. Megan attempted to push past Carlos and reach for her car door. Carlos grabbed her arm. "Wait!" Carlos tried to interject. At that moment Megan became enraged. "How dare he grab her after all he has already put them through?" Megan slapped Carlos's hand as she continued to push past him and open her car door. "Get in the car Blake!" Megan shouted as she did the same. Blake opened his car door and attempted to get in. At that moment, Carlos became enraged. He was unwilling to go back to the agony of living without the two of them. Megan quickly sat in the driver's seat and was looking over her shoulder awaiting her son to sit so she could leave as quickly as possible. Carlos reached in his waste belt and grabbed the gun that he kept on him even when he was off duty, cocked it, and pulled the trigger shooting Megan in the side of the head. Carlos stumbled backwards stunned as if someone else had shot the mother of his child in front of him. Blake witnessed Carlos shoot his mother, let out a scream, and begin running as fast as he could back to the school building. "Blake!" Carlos shouted out to his son. Blake did not stop running nor slow in speed. Carlos shouted his son's name once more as he raised the gun in Blake's direction and pulled the trigger striking Blake once in the center of his back. The boy fell forward falling face down on the concrete parking lot. Carlos quickly dropped the gun and ran over to his son. He dropped to his knees and cradled his son in his arms. "No, No No!" Carlos screamed. "Why did you run from me, I am your father, why did you run from me?!" Carlos repeated. "I'm so sorry son. Daddy loves you!" "I'm' so sorry!" Carlos said as he held Blake and watched as the boy took his last breath. "NOOOOOOOOOOOO!" Carlos yelled. With tears streaming down his face Carlos placed his son on the sidewalk and walked back to where he had dropped the gun. He could hear sirens in the background as he picked the gun up off the ground. He looked at Megan slouched over in the driver's side of her car with blood running down her head, neck, and chest, then looked back over at Blake bleeding all over the side walk. Carlos thought to himself, "What kind of man could kill his own family?" "I'm not worthy to live." Carlos thought as he put the gun to his head and pulled the trigger.

Christopher

Christopher sat in a small cell on a bed that was more like a cot. They had put him on suicide watch after processing, because Christopher was overly emotional. He could barely speak without crying. All he could think about was the indefinite circumstance of being away from his family. He could not bear the fact that his children might grow up like him, fatherless. When Christopher did speak, the deputies that processed him could barely make out what he was saying. Being away from his wife and kids was proving to be too much for him. Today was the day of his arraignment, and the day he would be charged for his crime. Christopher was ready to face his fate and get it over with. He was trying to emotionally prepare himself for the long road ahead, but he was having a tough time accepting that this was his new reality. Just a few mornings ago he was lying in bed with his beautiful wife and now he was in an empty holding cell. Christopher was now numb and just staring off into space. Because his thoughts had become too painful, his brain had moved him into survival mode to preserve the physical and mental state he had left.

Christopher was led into the courtroom wearing shackles and handcuffs. He kept his head down, as to not make eye contact with anyone. He was ashamed of his actions. He wished he hadn't gone out that night. He thought to himself that if he ever saw the light of day again he would spend all his days and nights with his wife and kids. No more hanging out in bars for him. The bailiff guided Christopher, to a podium in the center of the courtroom that came up to Christopher's chest. The judge was straight ahead of him. She was an older Caucasian female, she had a friendly face, but that didn't bring Christopher any comfort. Whether the judge was friendly or not, Christopher was not expecting any type of mercy.

Christopher could see that there were others in the court room at the time, but it was all a blur to him. The only person that mattered in the room was the judge. The judge begun by asking Christopher to state his full name. The judge then read out loud the charges Christopher was facing, to the tune of eight felonies. Christopher's heart sunk into his stomach. He was sure this was the end of him. He did not see the point of praying, because he had a relationship with God over the years, still, he didn't think that this was something he could pray his way out of. All his prayers since this ordeal began, were for the recovery of the man he hit and on his family's behalf. He had prayed for God to lessen their pain, they had done nothing at all to deserve what he was putting them through.

The judge finished reading off the charges and then called Christopher's name, "Mr. Davis," she says. "The document says that you left the scene of an accident, why did you leave Mr. Davis?" "I was afraid." Christopher answered. "It was an accident, I didn't know what to do, so I left." Christopher continued. The judge responded. "Nevertheless, Mr. Davis, accident or not you have committed a major offense, eight felonies to be exact." The judge continued. "You will be notified by your attorney of a date for your plea hearing".

Christopher was escorted back to his cell. He was informed that he would be transferred into the general population of the jailhouse by the end of the day. Christopher was nervous. He had never been to jail and did not know what to expect. His only point of reference were the shows and movies he saw on television about the correctional system. Christopher begin to pray for himself, he asked God to keep him safe through this ordeal. He was already worried about being away from his family, he did not want to die in jail and devastate his family even further. Christopher's new focus was survival. He didn't know what to expect or what was coming.

Antonette

Weeks had passed since Christopher turned himself in to the detective for the "Hit and run" accident. Antonette spent her days keeping herself busy with college and the kids. She even started going to the gym. Working out helped Antonette to clear her mind. She learned very quickly that too much idle time caused her mind to wander with negative thoughts. She would worry about the outcome of her husband's case and it threatened to depress her. She needed to be as positive as she could be, so she could continue to be the type of mother that she could be proud of.

The news about the accident had spread throughout the community and all of Christopher and Antonette's family members and friends now knew that

Christopher was the person responsible for the "Hit and run." The man Christopher hit, (Henry Taylor) was still in a coma and his injuries were serious, however, he was breathing on his own and in stable condition. Antonette got updates from her neighbor who was a nurse at the hospital. They were keeping a close eye on his condition because they knew if Henry died, that Christopher's charges would change to include "vehicular homicide". Antonette, her family, and Christopher's family all were praying for Henry's recovery on a daily basis.

Antonette began adjusting to her new normal without Christopher. They would talk daily when Christopher called her and the kids from jail. He would call in the afternoon and at bedtime to say goodnight. It wasn't much, however, Antonette looked forward to the calls from Christopher because it gave her peace of mind that he was okay. Antonette was grateful for what traces of their relationship she had left. They were awaiting Christopher's plea hearing, so Christopher had to stay in jail since there was no bond. The future was uncertain for them both, the only thing they were sure of was their commitment to each other.

Christopher

Christopher was trying his best to adjust to life in jail. He stayed to himself most days, however he would have short conversations with guards and other inmates about schedules and rules. He was learning to adapt and needed to know the "ins" and "outs" of "jail life". Christopher still struggled with the fact that he hurt someone, and that man was still in a coma. He felt worthless. The only thing that kept Christopher going was thinking of his wife and kids. His faith was non-existent at this point for he did not feel that God could exist in a place like this. He was aware of the fights and drama inside the jail, however Christopher remained far removed from any type of drama that occurred on the inside. The inmates played cards, dominoes, watched TV, and occasionally went outside for exercise. Christopher had yet to participate in any activities because his emotional state inhibited him from wanting to move. He was depressed. Christopher was just existing.

One day while outside in the yard, Christopher saw a young man playing basketball that seemed strangely familiar to him. Christopher mindlessly began to walk in his direction, all the while never taking his eyes off the man. Christopher felt as though his body had been hacked like a computer, and he was no longer in control of his legs. He felt a slight apprehension but could not stop moving in the man's direction. It was as though he was being drawn to him like a magnet. All fear was gone from Christopher as he continued to get closer and closer to the basketball court where the man was playing basketball. He never expected to see anything or anyone familiar to him for quite a while. However, on this day, he was being drawn to the basketball court by a strong feeling of familiarity. As Christopher got closer to the man, he began to make out characteristics. The closer he got the more he was drawn and the more familiar the man became. Christopher moved fearlessly closer and closer to try and see the man's face. Christopher walked around the basketball court until he ended up standing side by side with the basketball goal. He stood next to the goal but outside of the line where the other inmates were playing. He waited as the man turned with the ball and ran towards the basket again. As the man did, he and Christopher locked eyes, the man dropped the ball and ran over to Christopher. It was Christopher's younger uncle (Stephen). Stephen was about five years younger than Christopher. He had lived a life of crime and spent most of his teenage years behind bars. Unlike Christopher, Stephen was spoiled. Even though they had grown up in the same household, they had very different experiences. Stephen's biological mother was Christopher's grandmother. Stephen was the youngest of all the children that grew up in the home. Stephen was a "hothead". He was used to getting everything he wanted and when he didn't he would take it. His mother was very soft hearted when it came to Stephen due to the guilt she felt of not being able to give him the life she wanted for him. She had to raise four other children that were not hers, which stretched her finances out to nearly nothing. She had also left Stephen's father when he was still in pampers due to that same temper that Stephen had inherited.

The two men hugged each other tight, as if they were trying to squeeze the breath from one another. They were so grateful to have someone in this dreadfully lonely place that they had become oblivious to the other inmates surrounding them and awaiting the continuance of the game. The other inmates watched, some becoming emotional knowing that whatever was happening in front of them had something to do with these men finding an uncommon solace in this hellish place. No one was in a rush to break up this reunion. The inmates all watched in admiration of the love they could clearly see between the two men. Christopher had not seen Stephen since he moved out of his grandmother's home at sixteen years of age. At that time, his uncle was only eleven, and could not quite understand why Christopher had to leave. Christopher was ready to find his manhood and earn respect as an adult. The two were more like brothers. When Christopher left home, Stephen spiraled out of control. He started getting into fights at school, stealing, and talking back to his mother. Stephen had a void in his life due to not having a father. Christopher was the closest thing to a male role model that Stephen had. He was angry at Christopher for leaving, but Stephen had gotten to a place where he was finding his own manhood and finally understood why Christopher left. There was no longer any tension as far as Stephen was concerned. They were together again and that was all that mattered to him.

The two men finally broke their embrace. Tears were streaming down both of their faces. They had so many questions as to why either of them was in there. In that moment, their questions did not matter. All they knew was that they were happy to no longer be alone and have someone on the inside, for only someone on the inside could truly understand what they were experiencing.

Stephen and Christopher walked away from the basketball court both sniffling as they dried their tears, nevertheless overjoyed. Stephen had completely forgotten he was involved in the basketball game. The moment he saw Christopher, earth shifted for him and he knew that this moment of reconciliation was probably one of the most important moments of his young life. As the two men walked away, the other inmates picked up the basketball and continued the game.

Christopher and Stephen arrived at the picnic tables twenty yards from the basketball court. They both sat down with tears still in their eyes. "When did you….?" "What did you….?" both men attempted to speak at the same time, and then broke into laughter realizing that they both had the same questions for each other.

Christopher hadn't been in contact with Stephen because once Christopher had settled in his life with Antonette he had been told that Stephen ran away from home and was living on the streets. He had attempted to contact Stephen by leaving his number at several of Stephens' friend's houses but never got a call. Christopher was busy providing a stable life for his family. Since him and Antonette were teenage parents they were preoccupied with their own lives. Christopher hadn't forgotten about Stephen. He thought of him often. He thought that Stephen would always be okay because he had a mother who loved him unconditionally. Something Christopher knew nothing about, but felt Stephen was better off than he.

Christopher was wrong, Stephen had not even come close to stabilizing his own life. The only structure Stephen experienced was in the correctional system. He had been in and out of jail for the last six years.

The two men caught up on the last ten years. They were surprised to find out how many times they had tried to find one another. They had missed each other "by a hair" many times, so they concluded that the timing wasn't right. They were so happy to be reunited, that neither of them minded that the event was taking place inside of a jail. Christopher felt almost as if he could relive all the pain he had endured the past few weeks, if it was going to lead up to this moment again. Over the next couple of days, they were inseparable. A few times, Christopher started to believe that he could survive in jail having his little brother by his side.

Inherently, Christopher knew that this reunion had to take place due to the healing he and his brother were receiving from this encounter. He began to wonder about the intentionality of it all. Christopher believed in God, but this reunion helped to build Christopher's trust more than he thought possible. How could a horrific accident lead to something so beautiful? He now knew that whatever is supposed to be, will be.

Megan, Blake, and Carlos

Megan opened her eyes, her body felt heavy. She looked around as far as her neck could turn to see that she was in a hospital room. She felt confused. "Why am I in a hospital bed?" Megan thought. Her mind raced as she tried to recall what lead to her being hospitalized. "Was I in a car accident?" Megan thought. Megan thought about Blake and immediately tried to get out of bed. Her body would not move. She began to panic because she could not move and wanted to know where Blake was. A few moments later Megan's mom Diane entered the room. She walked over to Megan realizing that after two weeks of being in a coma, Megan was awake. "Oh my God!" "Megan you're awake!" Her mother shrilled. Diane's excitement quickly diminished when she remembered that Blake died at the scene of the shooting and she would have to tell Megan.

"Mom?" Megan began. "Why am I in the hospital?" "Where's Blake?" Megan's questions were coming back to back and a lump began growing in Diane's throat, she felt nauseated. "How do you tell someone that their child is dead?" Diane thought. Diane felt guilt at her own relief that Megan could speak and was not brain dead, however wanted to somehow become invisible so she would not have to have this conversation. Megan was anxiously looking up into her mother's eyes and Diane had not rehearsed what to say and was having trouble speaking. She began stroking Megan's hair as tears welled up in her eyes. "What is it mom?" "Is Blake okay?" Megan said trying to be calm all the while feeling like something was not right. "Why was Blake not here?" she thought. Her mother was the only person she allowed to keep Blake and if he wasn't with her mother something must be terribly wrong. Diane felt an overwhelming since of sadness realizing that not only did Megan not know her son was dead, but she had no memory of being shot by Carlos.

Diane begin to speak while her hand was still resting on the top of Megan's head. "Sweetie, there was a shooting." "Carlos," she paused. "Carlos shot you both and killed himself Megan." Blake died at the scene." They couldn't save him baby." "I'm so sorry." "We are going to get through this." Diane said in a whisper. "What?" Megan replied to her mother. "What are you saying?" "That doesn't make any sense." Megan said calmly. At that moment Megan's memory began to come back. She stopped speaking as she stared up at the ceiling replaying what she could remember. She remembered the balloons and Blake clinging tightly to her leg. Then she recalled the tussle between her and Carlos when she tried to get into her car. Megan did not recall seeing a gun but remembered the feeling of bewilderment at Carlos's proposal. She began to hyperventilate realizing that her mother was telling the truth. Megan wept in her hospital bed silently because her body was too weak to express the sadness and regret she felt. She could only imagine how confused and alone her son felt in the last moments of his life. Blake did not deserve what happened to him. Megan wished that she could just die right in her hospital bed. The pain was too much to bear. If she could move, she would have probably jumped off the roof of the hospital she thought. It was probably a mercy from God that she could not move, Megan thought. Or she would surely harm herself. She laid there feeling every bit of the pain she felt she deserved to feel. Megan felt as though she did not protect her child. It was her only job as a mom and she failed. Now her only child was gone.

Megan thought to herself that she would never recover from this. The next few days Megan did not eat or sleep. She laid in her hospital bed and stared out of the window. Thinking about all the mistakes she made and things she wished she could have done differently. The doctor told Megan that she would have to relearn to walk, use her arms, and hands again. Megan did not know where she would get the strength to achieve such a feat. She laid there feeling numb and empty. Her mother's heart broke for her, she wanted to comfort Megan but nothing she did could make up for the loss of her child. Megan asked her mother to leave her alone, but her mother would continue to come to the hospital every day and attempt to take care of her. Diane felt hopeless. She prayed for Megan to find peace during her pain.

Antonette

Restoration

Antonette sat on her living room floor with her two young children. The kids were playing with toys while Antonette folded clothes and watched television. The three began to feel a sense of normalcy. Antonette made sure the kids always had fun. The kids would even speak to their dad on the phone when he would call from jail. Antonette told the kids that their father was away working. Christopher told Antonette that he found his little brother in jail and has been enjoying catching up together. Antonette was thankful for the small blessings as well as the great ones. She could see how God was helping them along their way. Antonette and

Christopher were still awaiting his plea hearing. The court appointed lawyer, as well as Christopher were keeping her updated on possible dates for Christopher's hearing. The couple was not anxious at all to rush this process, they were told that the date could be months away due to a large volume of criminal cases in their town.

A delayed plea hearing did not bother Antonette because she was in no hurry to see Christopher be shipped off to prison. So, despite the current conditions the couple had found unexpected peace, that they would have never thought possible in their situation.

As Antonette sat on the floor folding laundry, she noticed a story on the news. She saw a picture of a man that looked very familiar to her. Antonette quickly grabbed the remote and turned up the television. The story was about Detective Gonzalez. The same detective that came to question her and picked up Christopher when he turned himself in. His picture was on the news because he had shot his family and killed himself. Antonette could not believe what she was seeing and hearing. The news went on to say that the only survivor was the mother involved. This news shocked Antonette. She called her sister to share the news. Antonette's heart was racing, as she wondered if this tragic incident would affect Christopher case. She was mortified that she had been in contact with the detective multiple times and he was capable of murdering his own family. Antonette thought to herself that you never know what people are going through, things are never really what they seem. She recalled how calm, direct, and seemingly in control the detective was when he came to question her. Antonette closed her eyes, she whispered to herself. "What is happening Lord?" She knew deep down that a shift had taken place that would set a new chain of events in motion. Antonette waited for Christopher to call later that night so she could reveal the news to him.

Christopher

Christopher had begun to socialize more. After reuniting with Stephen, he felt he had a second birth. He had a peace and a joy that he would not have thought in a million years was possible inside of a jail. One day while sitting in the recreation room where the inmates would play cards and watch television, Christopher was playing dominoes with Stephen and some of the other inmates. Christopher's back was to the television, but Stephen was on his team was sitting right across from him. While playing dominoes, Stephen noticed a story on the news about a murder /suicide that happened in their town. "Turn that up!" Stephen called out to the guard who had the remote to the television. All the men at the table including Christopher, turned to watch the news. It was a story on Detective Gonzales. "Hey Christopher," Stephen said. "Isn't that the detective that brought you in?" Unknown to Christopher at the time, Antonette was watching the exact same news story.

The murder happened two weeks ago, however they had been so caught up in Christopher's case that they were oblivious that the detective on his case had shot his family and committed suicide. "I think so." Christopher answered, feeling like he had just seen a ghost. Christopher's head was in a haze. "How could a man kill his own son?" Christopher thought. This story was too close to home, and even closer to Christopher's case. Christopher wondered if this would have any effect on his investigation. The detective was dead, and he oversaw Christopher's case. "Looks like you have a guardian angel my friend," said Stephen. "What do you mean?" asked Christopher. "The investigation is gonna take a hit Bro!" Stephen replied. Christopher was stunned. He was scared and nervous, his thoughts were racing. What if this new development prolonged his case? "It might be years before I get to go to court now," Christopher thought. He was sure that this was going to affect his case, he just wasn't sure how.

That night Christopher called Antonette for their usual goodnight chat. They both discussed how anxious the news about the detective made them. It was sad to them that a child was killed. They both could feel and understand the pain the mother must feel losing her child. That night they both said a prayer for the family of the murder suicide, before going to bed.

The next day Christopher was scheduled to meet with his lawyer. Christopher was escorted by guards to the conference room where his lawyer sat. He was a Caucasian man, very thin, with light blonde hair that he wore slicked back. His hair was slightly thinning which is why he probably wore it back. His face and features were also thin. He had on a dark blue suit and glasses. His glasses were thin gold frames. He stood when Christopher entered the room extending his hand as Christopher approached the table. "How are you Christopher?" the lawyer asked. "I'm good," Christopher responded quickly shaking the lawyer's hand. Christopher was anxious to get to the subject at hand. He wasn't in the mood for small talk considering that his own life was still hanging in the balance. The man he hit was still in a coma. That was good news because he was alive. If the man was living, Christopher felt as if there would be a chance for him to get out of jail. "Christopher," the lawyer began. "I have a plea deal ready for you," the lawyer said. "Because you are a first-time offender, I was able to get you a great deal from the D.A.'s office." Christopher listened as his lawyer continued. "I was able to convince them to let you plea to leaving the scene only." "Lab reports came back, and this guy was heavily intoxicated when he walked out in front of your car." "Apparently, he has been hit before." "It's like he plays in the street," the lawyer chuckled. "So, because of that, I was able to get you five to ten Christopher." "Five to ten?!" Christopher asked sounding shocked. "My kids won't even remember me!" Christopher added. "You don't have many options Christopher". The lawyer replied, "We need to plea this thing out before this guy dies." "If this man dies, you will be looking at a lot worse Christopher," the lawyer added. "But you said yourself that the guy was drunk, this wasn't even my fault!" Christopher exclaimed starting to become emotional. "Christopher the most you will probably do is five years." "You could possibly be released early for good behavior." the lawyer added. "Possibly?!" Christopher responded. "You want me to base my decision on a possibility?!" said Christopher becoming more agitated.

Christopher felt dismayed. He knew the deal was good considering what he had done. "Look, just take a day or two and think it over." "I will try to get a better deal, but I think they were generous enough considering there is a man in the hospital fighting for his life because of you," the lawyer warned." "You left a man dying in the street Christopher," the lawyer replied. "You can't expect to just walk away from something like this!" Christopher put his head down. He was feeling pressure to take the deal. The guilt was almost unbearable. A small voice in Christopher's head would not allow him to take the deal. He was not willing to sign his life away that easily. Since the man he hit had been drunk, Christopher felt he may have better chances fighting this in court. Also, Christopher knew that he had to discuss it with his wife first. "I will think about it," Christopher said before getting up from the table to leave the meeting with his lawyer. Christopher knew this day was coming, however it was becoming real now that he could see clearly that prison might be in his future. The thought alone was so painful that Christopher started to feel like he did the first day he entered the jail. Seeing his brother on the inside had distracted him for a while, now the reality of his true circumstances were all rushing back at once.

Megan

Megan felt an immense amount of pain in her arms and legs as she dragged her body through the railings at her physical therapy session. Her face was wet with sweat as she fell backwards into her wheelchair. "You can't keep giving up," her therapist encouraged. "I don't care if I never walk again." "Take me back to my room please!" Megan snapped. "Do you wanna try one more time?" "I will hold you this time?" the therapist questioned. "No!" Megan shouted. Megan was now living in the same hospital where she once worked. Everyone was so supportive. The doctors and nurses were all coming to visit her in her hospital room. She was surrounded by flowers, balloons, and greeting cards. However, there was no comfort in anything or anyone for Megan. Everything in her life was a reminder that her son was gone, and she was the cause of it. Megan sat in her room daily, not watching television or looking out of the window. She felt unworthy of any joy in life. Her normally chubby frame had become thin and frail. She kept her hair pulled back and only showered when the nurses forced her to. Her only sense of peace is when she thought about ways to take her own life. She sat in a dark hospital room day in and day out fantasizing about her own death. She had convinced herself that there was no God. She would either kill herself when she left the hospital or live the rest of her days without meaning and bitter. Megan decided it was better to die than to put her mother through the trouble of taking care of her.

Megan's mother was coming to get her in a few days when she was released from the hospital. Megan was still undecided on how she would take her own life. She tried to think of the best way to lessen the trauma on her mother and concluded that she could not. Her mother was going to be devastated no matter how Megan chose to take her life. Megan pondered slitting her wrists in the tub, overdosing on pain pills, or carbon monoxide poisoning. She knew that she would have to become physically stronger if she was going to get to the garage and crank the car. Megan had no desire to become stronger, so she could not take her life that way. She wanted to end her life as soon as possible because she did not want any life without Blake. Megan decided that the best way to die and not be revived was to overdose at bedtime. Her mom would be checking on her regularly, but if she thought Megan was asleep she would let her die unknowingly.

Megan knew that her mother was strong, and she would pray her way through it like she does everything. Her mother had a hard life and had become accustomed to loss. Megan thought to herself that her mother would get over the loss of her just the same. She was at peace with her decision.

Christopher and Antonette

Antonette left the gym and headed to the grocery store. Christopher had been gone a little over a month now. Antonette wondered how the death of the detective would affect Christopher's case. There was still no court date, but Christopher told her that the attorney wanted him to plead guilty to a lesser charge. Antonette advised Christopher not to take the deal. She felt that God was not through with their situation. Antonette believed that God was too good to allow Christopher to serve five to ten years. She knew in her heart that he was still able to change this situation. The couple refused to give up hope until there was nothing else in their power they could do. Antonette used their savings to get another lawyer. She and

Christopher both no longer trusted his court appointed lawyer. They felt as if he was trying to please the district attorney's office with the last plea deal. Antonette did not think it was much of a deal at all. She prayed for mercy and the deal he brought back, did not feel much like mercy to the couple.

Antonette finished her grocery shopping and headed to pick up the children from her sister's house. She drove along singing to gospel music in her minivan. She was happy that her mother raised her with strong Christian values, or she would not have the strength for a journey this long. Even though she was not happy about her and Christopher's current situation, she felt as if she had been prepared for it somehow.

Antonette pulled up to her sister's house. Her sister and the children were outside playing in the front yard. Antonette got out of her van. Her sister greeted her with a grin, "Guess what?" Erin said sounding bubbly. "Henry Taylor came out of his coma today!" she said sounding excited. Antonette closed her eyes and silently thanked God. She took it as a sign that everything was going to be okay. "They are charging him with jay-walking." Erin continued. "Wow," Antonette responded. "That's actually good news, maybe now Chris will get a better deal!" Antonette exclaimed. "Maybe!" replied Erin.

The two women gathered up the children and put them into the van. Antonette felt a sense of peace. She did not know how, but she had a feeling that everything was going to be okay. Things were changing gradually and Antonette continued to pray prayers of thanks and plead for mercy. She felt God's grace every day. Her and her sister hugged, then

Antonette left to go home and prepare dinner for her children. She smiled to herself on the drive home. "I know you are working," Antonette said to God as she pulled up in her driveway.

Antonette awoke later than usual the next morning to a missed call on her phone. She did not hear the phone ring, she thought to herself. Antonette didn't recognize the number so she listened to the voicemail. It was Mrs. Jones at the district attorney's office. She had left Antonette an urgent message. Antonette became anxious. She was hoping for good news, but with all the bad news they had received regarding Christopher's case in the past, she was slightly nervous.

Antonette called the number back and asked to speak to Mrs. Jones. There was a long hold and then Mrs.

Jones came to the phone. "Mrs. Davis," said Mrs. Jones. "How are you?" "I am good." Antonette replied with hesitation in her voice. "Well I was calling to inform you that we have to drop the charges against your husband Mr. Davis." Antonette's heart was racing. "Is this some kind of cruel joke?" she thought to herself. She would have asked it out loud if she hadn't called the number back herself. "What, how?" Antonette asked the district attorney. "Well the investigating detective has passed away, and we were unable to find any documented evidence related to Mr. Davis's case." "We cannot proceed prosecuting a case with no evidence," said Mrs. Jones dryly. "Oh My God, are you serious!" Antonette exclaimed not believing her ears. "Unfortunately yes," replied Mrs. Jones in a very dry voice. "He will still be charged with leaving the scene of an accident, which is a misdemeanor, and for that he will get time served." "Your husband will be released into your custody today," said the district attorney.

Antonette feared that she could possibly be dreaming, as this was truly a modern-day miracle for her family. "Oh my God!" exclaimed Antonette. I cannot believe this is really happening!" Antonette said, beginning to cry. "Take care," replied Mrs. Jones before hanging up the phone.

Antonette laid in her bed stunned. She cried tears of happiness. She had never felt the love of God more strongly than she did at that very moment. She felt as though God had broken every rule just for her and her family and it was truly a miracle. Antonette did not know how to feel. Christopher coming home did not seem real to her. For almost two months, he only existed on the phone and through letters. To have her husband back home would be the greatest blessing she could ever imagine. "Thank you, God!" Antonette cried out. "Thank you, thank you, thank you!" Antonette put her head down and thanked God more times than she could count. She was still having difficulty processing what just occurred. She then began to wonder if Christopher knew yet......

Christopher sat in the cafeteria with his brother Stephen at the table with several other men. They made jokes and laughed as if they were on the outside. The guard repeatedly told the men to quiet down. As they became louder than the allowed jail volume. Christopher did not have a clue of when he was getting out of jail. He and Antonette had decided to turn down the last plea deal and fight his case in court. He had begun to make the best out of his situation. He and Stephen would spend their days playing basketball, cards, or just reminiscing about the fun times of their childhood. Sometimes they would discuss the unpleasant memories. Christopher had a lot of unresolved pain from his childhood. He felt a sense of comfort that even though Stephen did not understand, he would still listen and allow Christopher to voice his hurt about his feelings about their upbringing. Although they were bought up in the same house, their experiences were drastically different.

After breakfast Stephen decided to go and socialize with the other inmates while Christopher stayed in his cell and read. A guard came shortly after Stephen left the cell. "The sheriff would like to meet with you," the guard said. "The Sheriff?" Christopher asked sounding confused. "Yes, the sheriff," the guard repeated sarcastically. Christopher gathered himself, and hesitantly followed the guard down the long dim hall. The jail was noisy with all the other inmate's random conversations and numerous games being played. Christopher was nervous and scared. "What could the sheriff possibly want with me?" Christopher thought. The closer the two men got to the sheriff's office the more nervous Christopher became. They entered one of the locked doors and it closed behind them. At that moment, Christopher realized that he is usually handcuffed when he is brought beyond the jail doors. Christopher's' thoughts really began to race at that point, wondering what in the world was happening. The two men reached an office right before the front doors of the jail. Christopher thought to himself that he could make a run for it at that point and wondered why he was being given so much trust. His curiosity was burning now. The guard opened the door to the sheriff's office and ushered Christopher inside. "Have a seat please" the sheriff said looking down at his desk. "Do you know why you are here Mr. Davis?" the Sheriff asked. "No sir," Christopher responded. "Well," said the sheriff. "I've received a call this morning like no other call I have received in my 30 years of being a sheriff and this is my fourth jail." The sheriff continued. "Okay," Christopher said feeling intrigued and less frightened at that point. "The District Attorney's office called this morning and they have to dismiss your whole case." Christopher's mouthed dropped open, "Really?!" Christopher exclaimed almost jumping out of his chair. "Apparently, the detective on your case blew his brains out and misplaced your evidence." "So, Mr. Davis, you are free to go," the sheriff said as he extended his hand towards the door. "Well after processing of course," the Sheriff said with a chuckle. Christopher shook the sheriff's hand still in disbelief. Tears were streaming down his face as he continued to sit in the chair in the sheriff's office. The Sheriff and the guard were talking, both marveling in amazement at the news. Christopher put his head down and prayed. "Wow God!" Christopher said to himself. "I can't believe I'm going home," he whispered to himself. "Is there anyone you would like to call Mr. Davis?" the Sheriff asked. "Maybe a ride?" the sheriff added. "My wife," Christopher said in a whisper. He was feeling so many emotions that he could barely speak. Christopher could barely believe what was happening. One minute he had an indefinite amount of time to serve, and the next, he was just being released with no more charges and no questions asked. Christopher was in awe of God. He wasn't sure he believed in miracles until this very moment. Christopher was living in a real-life miracle. The sheriff handed Christopher his personal cell phone and Christopher called Antonette. She answered on the first ring because she had been awaiting his call. They both cried tears of joy, when Antonette revealed that she had gotten the same call that morning. Christopher said he would be released in an hour and Antonette promised to be there waiting when he got out.

Megan

The day had arrived for Megan to be released from the hospital. She had begun to move around a bit more in her hospital room, but still needed her wheel chair for distances longer than ten feet. She gathered her belongings and was lying in bed looking at pictures of Blake. She missed him so much her heart physically ached. She was unable to say goodbye because she was still in a coma when Blake was laid to rest at his funeral. All Megan wanted was to die and be with her son. She would have taken her life already but feared that she would be discovered too quickly in her hospital room and revived by the doctors and nurses. Megan knew that she had to wait until she was released from the hospital.

.

Over the course of the day, the nurses and doctor were all coming in to say goodbye to her. Megan tried her best to be friendly and not show the amount of self-loathing that she was feeling. Her mother arrived around lunch time, came in and asked if Megan was ready to go. She was ready to get the day over with knowing she had a secret that was going to end all her suffering.

The nurse came into the room to help Megan into her wheelchair. Megan noticed her mother was oddly in a "chipper" mood and it annoyed her. She thought to herself that her mother was trying to be upbeat in hopes that it would cheer Megan up. Her mother rambled on and on about her plans for them the next couple of days. Megan tuned her mother out and could not make sense of anything she said. The nurse pushed Megan down the halls of the hospital in her wheelchair towards the lobby. Megan gazed into each room they passed wondering about the person's situation inside and wishing she could be any of them rather than herself. Just then they arrived in the lobby, Megan was staring out through the lobby windows, the sun was shining bright. It did not make a difference to Megan as she could no longer take her son to the park, or the swimming pool. "Life was truly worthless," Megan thought to herself. The wheelchair stopped moving and Megan felt the nurse's hands on the sides of her shoulders. Megan wondered why the nurse had stopped pushing the wheelchair. They had been sitting in the same spot for over a minute. She stopped gazing out of the window and looked straight ahead. There was a large group of kindergarteners and a few teachers standing in front of the doors of the hospital. They were holding a banner with Blake's picture and "We Love You!" written in big purple letters. Megan looked down at the ground and in that moment lost complete control of her emotions. The children crowded around and hugged her one by one. Some of them hugged her at the same time. The teachers had to keep reminding the children to let someone else take a turn. Megan felt each tiny hand grab her and heard each tiny voice say, "I love you." She felt the presence of Blake so strongly that she could not help but to sob uncontrollably.

The reminder of Blake was almost too much for Megan to bear. Once each child and teacher had hugged Megan, they presented her with the banner in Blake's honor. Megan had a very difficult time composing herself. She felt so many emotions but most importantly, she felt gratitude that the teachers had organized this field trip for Blake's class to come and greet her as she was being released from the hospital.

When Megan was finally able to compose herself, she thanked the children and the teachers. She could barely speak as she had not used her voice much in weeks, but she could see how important it was to the children by the hopeful looks on their faces and the twinkle in each one of their little eyes. Every time a child hugged her it reminded her of Blake's little hands and arms when he hugged her. Megan was humbled. The feelings that Blake's class brought up in Megan reminded her that there was still life to be lived and feelings to be felt. Her grief was not gone, but Megan felt more meaning to her life than she felt since she had awoken from her coma.

On the drive home, Megan sobbed. She was overwhelmed by the love from Blake's class. She did not know it was possible to feel the spirit of her son through other children. She began to feel that Blake was still with her. She knew that she would no longer be able to go through with her plan of taking her own life, as she did not want to disappoint the children from Blake's class. She thought to herself in that moment, if she was not going to commit suicide, she would have to find a way to keep living. Megan looked over at her mother who was driving, reached over, grabbed her hand, and squeezed it. Diane smiled as she squeezed back even harder. Despite the tough road ahead, both women realized that they were going to be okay.

Christopher and Antonette

Antonette sat outside the jailhouse in her van with CJ and Cadence, both in their car seats. She had butterflies in her stomach as if she was back in high school waiting on her crush to ask her to dance. She could not believe that the day was finally here, and Christopher was coming home for good. Antonette was in awe of God. She felt in her heart that there was truly no limit to what God could do. She remembered the prayer she made the day the swat team took Christopher away in handcuffs. She always believed in God, but never in a million years could she have imagined Christopher's release in this way. Antonette felt horrible that another family suffered such a tragic loss. She and Christopher could understand the pain the mother must be experiencing since their own son is around the age of the little boy whom was murdered. However, Antonette was certain that the two families were destined to cross paths. God had used that tragedy to bring Antonette's family back together. Antonette felt in her heart that God had a greater purpose for her and her family's future because they had been given a second chance. Antonette was filled with joy and the love of God.

Antonette's excitement to see her husband was so intense that she could not contain it. She decided to get out of the van and stand outside. Antonette had only been standing outside for a few minutes when she heard the doors of the jail open. As they did, she saw Christopher walking out with a huge grin on his face. Antonette grinned back as she walked towards him. The two finally reached each other and hugged tighter than they ever hugged each other in their lives.

The couple engaged in a long passionate kiss. This had been the first time they ever spent more than one night a part since they met. Antonette and Christopher wiped away tears as they walked hand in hand to the van. Christopher opened the back door to greet his children. He kissed them both on their cheeks and then jumped in the passenger side next to his wife. "Let's go home!" shouted Christopher. Antonette smiled as she pulled the van out of the parking lot. "Thank-you God," she whispered as she pulled onto the street and headed home.

Weeks had passed, and daily life had resumed back to normal for Christopher and Antonette. Antonette was focusing on finishing her degree and Christopher was working hard to continue to save up money for the house he wanted to buy for his family. It was a Friday afternoon, Antonette was preparing dinner in the kitchen, while Christopher sat in the living room watching the news. A story came on about the rape of a twelve-year old girl. Christopher sat up in his chair as he watched the police escort an entire family from a house. Christopher took notice because one of the family members was in a wheelchair. He called out to Antonette to come and watch the story with him. Christopher was not a big fan of the news as he felt that news depressed people. He felt that he could be more focused on the positive aspects of life when he did not watch the news. When he did watch, he mostly watched the weather. However, on this day, this particular news story was calling out to him for some reason. Christopher could not take his eyes off the television screen. He was particularly drawn to the man in the wheelchair. Antonette was now standing next to him as the news switched screens.

On the next screen were mug shots of each adult in the home that had been arrested and charged with the rape. One of the names underneath a picture was "Henry Taylor." His charges were aggravated sexual battery, and incest. Christopher and Antonette stared in silence as they watched. They were both speechless as they realized that the man in the wheelchair was the same man that Christopher had hit three months ago. The couple did not speak one word, as they turned and stared at each other. Christopher's mind raced. He began to wonder if the accident he had been carrying around guilt for was an accident at all. Christopher felt that he could have been chosen to carry out a greater plan. He nor Antonette knew what it all meant, nevertheless they both felt a greater sense of peace towards the three-month ordeal they had just gone through. From that point on, everything in life had purpose, nothing was meaningless for the couple…{THE END}

The (Davis) Williams Family 2004

Credits

Written by

Chantwaun C. Williams

Co Authors

Tamir H. Williams Sr. (Christopher)

Prophetess Demetrice A. Williams, (Antonette), In association with New Harvest Ministries.

Graphic Designer

Michael Corvin (Ukraine)

Special Thanks!

Special thanks to Tamir and Demetrice Williams for trusting and believing in me enough to write their testimony. Everyone needs someone to believe in their dreams.

C.C.W

Made in the USA
Columbia, SC
23 December 2019